BECAUSE GOD DON'T MAKE NO JUNK.

Research for this publication was funded by the U.S. Department of Education's Fund for the Improvement for Postsecondary Education under Grant G008302531.

The contents of the publication, however, do not necessarily reflect the views or policies of the U.S. Department of Education, nor does mention of institutions, publications, organizations and programs therein imply endorsements by the United States Government.

The grantee, Educational Access, Incorporated, and its professional staff are solely responsible for the contents of the publication.

Project Staff

Anna Leider, President   **Co-Project Director**
Educational Access, Inc., Alexandria, VA

Robert Leider, Educational Access, Inc.   **Co-Project Director**

Dr. Baltazar A. Acevedo, Jr., Director   **Senior Consultant**
Dallas Leadership Program, MALDEF,
Southern Methodist University, Dallas, TX

Mrs. Dorothea Slocum, Reference and Young Adult   **Senior Consultant**
Librarian, Washington, DC Public Library; Director and Founder,
Operation College-Bound, Washington, DC

Edward B. Wall, Dean of Admission & Financial Aid,   **Senior Consultant**
University of Southern California, Los Angeles, CA

Patricia L. Reid, Trinity College, Washington, DC   **Project Artist**

Thanks also go to Victoria Fabisch, Teresa Méndez-Faith, Marilyn Stokstad, and the staff of The Graphic Center, Inc.

A NOTE ON THE TITLE

The title is not original with us. It has been around for years as graffiti, either in the version we reproduced, or in variants thereof. The origins are unknown. It can be conjectured that the saying had its beginning in black churches, in the days before equal opportunity, affirmative action and civil rights. Its intent: to give people strength and pride when they could not draw strength and pride from laws and societal arrangements.

Inquiries should be addressed to **ANNA LEIDER, P.O. Box 3437, Alexandria, VA 22302. Telephone (703) 823-1882.**

ISBN 0-917760-69-7

PRINTED IN THE UNITED STATES OF AMERICA

Contents

Forward To Parents

Young people are the life blood of our society. With them comes the hope for better communities and a brighter future for all. The key to unlocking this brighter future is education—a college education.

Getting a job right out of high school may seem appealing to your child, or it may seem necessary in order for your family to make ends meet. But in the long run, it is not the best move for your child, or your family.

As technology continues to advance, the job market for unskilled labor continues to shrink. For someone without extra training or education, only dead end and low paying jobs will be available, if any at all. A college education changes that. It qualifies your child for a job with a future—one that pays well and is secure; one that benefits your community. America needs your children to become its teachers, its doctors and its lawyers.

A college education provides the skills and confidence your child will need to survive in this world; skills and confidence which are just as important for your daughter as they are for your son. Your daughter still has an important role as wife and mother, the essential link of the "familia," but today her role is complicated as she must also work to help pay her family's bills. A college education will enable her to contribute to her family as well as her community.

Let your child go away to school, even if it's far away from home. Don't think that your child will be alone and unprotected. College housing is carefully arranged, meal plans are well established, and support services of all types abound—especially for Black, Chicano and Latino ethnic groups. Going away to school will help your son or daughter mature and learn to deal effectively with all kinds of people. Going away to school will also strengthen family and community ties. No college wants its students to abandon their families or their cultural, ethnic and racial heritage. In fact, colleges encourage diversity in their student body as a means to promote better understanding amongst all people.

Don't let your financial situation prevent you from seeking a college education for your child. Money is available from the state and federal government and from any college your child wishes to attend. However, in order to receive this money, you must fill out an application form. These applications are available at your child's high school. The questions are sometimes complicated, but your child's guidance counselor will be able to help you. Remember, this form must be filled out, and filled out accurately, in order for you to receive financial assistance. College is expensive and almost no one is able to complete four years without this kind of assistance. The money is there for the benefit of your children. This is America's way of investing in its citizens and thereby investing in its future. There is nothing shameful about accepting it.

This booklet will explain the college admission and financial aid process in more detail. It will remove other concerns you may have. And it will tell you where to get the answers to any questions which remain unanswered. Read it. And give your child a future.

As a parent, your children respect you and want to please you. Encourage them. Help them make their dreams come true.

If you have babies, read to them. Answer their questions. Encourage their curiosity and their imagination.

Once your children begin school, encourage attendance and the completion of homework. Visit the school. Meet the teacher, the counselor. Be sure your child takes academic courses—math, science, english, social science, and a foreign language (encourage them to study Spanish).

If your child has been placed in a curriculum that is not college preparatory (i.e., business or vocational) you have the right to have it changed. Demand it.

Prefacio Para Los Padres

La juventud es la esperanza de nuestra sociedad. En ella reside la posibilidad de conseguir un futuro mejor para todos. Por eso, nuestros jovenes necesitan la oportunidad de prepararse bien para cumplir con sus responsibilidades; necesitan más educación—una educación universitaria o un programa de estudios técnicos.

Tal vez su hijo(a) piense trabajar inmediatamente después de terminar sus estudios secundarios. Quizás sea realmente necesario que trabaje para ayudar con los gastos familiares. Pero a largo plazo, el trabajar no es el mejor paso ni para su hijo(a) ni para su familia.

A medida que avanza la tecnología, disminuye la posibilidad de obtener trabajo para los obreros sin entrenamiento adecuado. Para un(a) joven sin educación universitaria o estudios técnicos, a menudo sólo hay trabajos que pagan poco y que no tienen posibilidades de ascenso. La educación universitaria puede cambiar eso totalmente ya que le da a su hijo(a) la oportunidad de obtener los mejores empleos y asegurarse una posición económica que beneficie tanto a su familia como a su comunidad. Este país necesita a sus hijos; ellos seran los líderes del futuro: como maestros, doctores, abodgados, comerciantes.

La educación universitaria da a sus hijos la competencia y la confianza necesarias para sobrevivir en el mundo competitivo actual, calificaciones ambas que son tan importantes tanto para su hija como para su hijo. Ésta todavía tiene un papel importante como esposa y madre, función esencial dentro de la familia; pero hoy día este papel se ha complicado porque ella tiene que trabajar para ayudar con los gastos de la casa. La educación universitaria hará posible que su hija contribuya activamente al bienestar de la familia y de la comunidad.

Es importante que ustedes permitan que sus hijos asistan a la universidad, aunque ésta esté lejos de su ciudad o pueblo. No crean que sus hijos estarán solos o sin protección. La universidad tiene habitaciones y planes de comida establecidos, y abundan los servicios y programas de ayuda. La vida en la universidad ayudará a su hijo(a). Allí aprenderá a convivir con otra gente. La experiencia universitaria de su hijo(a) también fortalecerá a la familia y a la comunidad. Ninguna universidad quiere que sus estudiantes abandonen sus lazos familiares u olviden su herencia étnica o cultural. De hecho, las universidades quieren que haya diversidad racial y cultural entre sus estudiantes a fin de promover un entendimiento mejor y mayor comprensión entre ellos.

Y no crean ustedes que su familia es demasiado pobre y que, por eso, su hijo(a) no puede asistir a la universidad. El gobierno federal y el gobierno en las diferentes estados tienen dinero para ayudar con los gastos de educación. También las universidades cuentan con fondos de ayuda financiera. Para recibir este dinero hay que completar un formulario de solicitud. (Pueden obtener un formulario en la escuela secundaria de su hijo o hija.) Si las preguntas parecen un poco complicadas, el (la) consejero(a) de su hijo(a) podrá ayudarlos. Recuerden que es preciso completar ese formulario correctamente para obtener el dinero. El costo de la enseñanza universitaria es muy alto y la mayoría de la gente no puede pagar sin este tipo de ayuda. El dinero existe y está allí para beneficio de sus hijos. El futuro de este país depende en gran parte de la educación de los jovenes. **No tengan ninguna vergüenza en aceptarlo.**

Este folleto explicará en detalle lo relacionado con el proceso de ingreso a la universidad y con la manera de obtener la ayuda económica necesaria.También discutirá otros aspectos de interés y les indicará dónde pueden obtener más información. Léanlo ciudadosamente y den a su hijo(a) la posibilidad de prepararse bien para su vida.

Los hijos respetan a sus padres y quieren satisfacerlos. Los padres deben guiar y aconsejar a sus hijos. Ayúdenlos a que sus sueños se hagan realidad.

Si tienen ninos aún pequeños, contesten sus preguntas y estimulen su curiosidad y su imaginacion.

Cuando su(s) hijo(s) comience(n) la escuela, asegúrense de que asista(n) regularmente a clase y que complete(n) sus tareas. Visiten la escuela y traten de conocer a su(s) maestro(s) y consejero(s). Asegúrense de que su hijo(a) siga cursos académicos: matemáticas, ciencias, inglés, historia, y alguna lengua extranjera (español, si es posible).

Si su hijo(a) ha sido colocad(a) en un programa vocacional o de negocios (en vez de estar en un programa de preparación para la universidad), ustedes, como padres, tienen todo el derecho de pedir un cambio. Si así lo quisieran, exijan el cambio lo antes posible.

Chapter 1

Martin Luther King, Jr., Matthew Henson, Charlotte Wilhite, and You

When you are young you may be judged by your clothes, by your music, by your haircut, and by how you talk.

But think about the older people who have really earned your respect, and why. Is it because of the way they look, or is it because of all the good things they have done for our society? Of course, there is Martin Luther King, Jr., but what about Matthew Henson, the black member of Admiral Perry's expedition who in 1909 planted the American flag at the North Pole. Or Phyllis Wheatley, a slave who in 1773 became the second woman to have a book published in the United States. And, Daniel Hale Williams, the doctor who in 1893 performed the first successful heart operation. Today, Thurgood Marshall is a Justice to the Supreme Court. Roberto Goizueta is chairman of Coca-Cola. Marion Barry is mayor of Washington, DC. Tom Bradley is mayor of Los Angeles. Henry Cisnero is mayor of San Antonio. Wilson Goode is mayor of Philadelphia. Maurice Ferré is mayor of Miami. Harold Washington is mayor of Chicago. Frederico Peña is mayor of Denver. And, Andrew Young is mayor of Atlanta. This list includes nearly every major city in the United States. Think about it. These men and women overcame great obstacles to earn the respect of an entire nation. You, too, can earn this respect by being:

- *The doctor who heals the sick.*
- *The scientist who finds a cure for cancer.*
- *The lawyer who defends the community.*

- *The coach who trains the winners.*
- *The architect who builds the city.*
- *The teacher who challenges students.*
- *The citizen who cares about the city and its residents.*
- *The parent who raises responsible children and provides for their future.*

You can be any of these people. Or an author, dentist, newscaster, computer programmer, accountant, pilot, librarian, engineer, or whatever else you want to be or dare to be.

It's your decision. But it's a decision you can't put off any longer. You must make it now, and make it **BY SETTING YOUR SIGHTS ON A COLLEGE EDUCATION.** That's the best way to get respect.

Every year, hundreds of thousands of people achieve the goal of a college degree. Are they different from you? NO! They are exactly like you—no better and no worse. They took the first step toward achievement, and so must you.

Will it be easy? Maybe yes. Probably no. Nothing worth doing is ever easy. Otherwise, everybody would be an astronaut or lawyer or doctor or engineer ... You will be the one who determines how easy or how hard the road will be, how light or how heavy the load. **YOU AND NO ONE ELSE!**

But cheer up. While the decision is yours alone, there is support and there is help. Turn to your parents, counselors, teachers. Tell them your plans, share your dreams. **REMEMBER: A LONG TRIP IS ALWAYS MORE FUN WHEN OTHERS GO WITH YOU.**

You probably didn't get an early start on college planning. You hadn't thought about the future. It didn't seem important. But it's not too late. It never is.

Now while you are thinking about it and questioning yourself, take the time to read on and learn how other young people took the first step toward a college education.

First meet Charlotte Wilhite, a sophomore at Wayne State University in Detroit:

"An education is not merely a functional system of becoming middle class, but an education makes one self-conscious, self-sufficient, and powerful ... An educated person can throw off the belief that he or she is a victim of a maze of uncontrollable forces."

Listen to Charlotte.

Read this booklet. Keep it close at hand. Follow its advice. It will help you get started on the road to achievement.

Chapter 2

Meet William Jackson: He Made It, And So Can You

You heard Charlotte Wilhite.

Now meet William Jackson, a young black engineer. His current project: the rehabilitation of an airport pavement in Pennsylvania.

While thinking about where he came from, where he is now, and how he got there, Mr. Jackson wrote this poem:

SURVIVAL

I often wonder why
In the time of crisis
Wise men seldom cry.

I think that if we cry
During the distress and strife
We could find the courage to try.

"But why try?" you may ask,
And it is your task
To survive,
Stay alive!

No one came to make your way
At night or even during the day;
So get out there and make them pay.

You owe it to yourself to pay your dues
And strive for the news
When you conquer your blues.

Survive, my brother; survive, my sister.
We will be free in time, "mister."

So be on your guard
'Cause the world is hard
And it looks for us to retard!

Mr. Jackson writes to you:

"*You may wonder how this poem relates to you—a person striving for an education. The essence of the poem is that an individual has to be aware of the factors which work against him or her if that person is to survive. Survival is a personal matter; the individual must measure and determine what is important and what is essential in order to succeed on a daily basis and make the quality of his or her life much better.*

"*We are all intuitive beings but we often let our emotions control us and consequently our lives. Through self-discipline I made myself conquer my bitterness because it would only inhibit my growth if I allowed it to. You must do the same to open your mind to your potential.*

"*A lot of young people are bitter, as I was, and this poison is a product of their environment and lack of self-esteem. I say to you, 'Admit that you are angry with yourself. You want to change. And you're going to make the investment of time, energy, and faith in yourself to overcome the barriers that stand in your way. Believe in yourself.'*

"*I know you are searching or else you wouldn't be reading my words. Today I am a successful engineer. I have my story. Now tell your story through your actions. Listen to those who can help you and keep your mind open as you prepare for college and your trip to self-esteem, growth and success.*

"*God Bless You.*"

William Jackson

Chapter 3
Good Reasons For Going To College

YOU STILL HAVE CHOICES

When you are young, you still have choices—choices which will determine what kind of life you will lead.

It can be a good life—one which sets your spirit free and turns dreams into reality.

Or it can be a frustrating life—one which leaves you to drift, powerless to control even your own destiny.

Make the right choice now. You still have the luxury of time; but time, once emptied, cannot be refilled like the gas tank of a car. Or, more poetically put:

Nothing can bring back the hour
Of splendour in the grass, of glory in the flower.
                                    —William Wordsworth

Now is the time—the right time—to prepare yourself for the adult roles which you can assume, which are your right to assume, and which society wants you to assume.

It is your life. Begin it with a college education. The rewards are guaranteed to be as abundant as the challenges.

WHAT COLLEGE DOES FOR YOU

In simplest terms, you can expect two things from your college experience—developed personal skills, and the core knowledge of an academic field, such as education or engineering. There is no wall between personal skills and occupational knowledge. They interact to bring you personal satisfaction and the self-confidence necessary to become a respected and contributing member of the community.

PERSONAL SKILLS

What are personal skills?

- Learning to learn.
- Learning to write and speak effectively.
- Learning to listen with care.
- Learning to analyze a problem.
- Learning to persuade others to your point of view.
- Learning to help others overcome problems.
- Learning to work with people from all backgrounds.
- Learning to set goals.
- Learning to manage time effectively.
- Learning to demonstrate initiative, make decisions.
- Learning to accept responsibility.
- Learning to deal with change.

OCCUPATIONAL KNOWLEDGE

A professional field, whether it is accounting, forestry, business, law, literature, or medicine is a specialized body of knowledge. That knowledge is acquired in a college classroom. The college degree is the passport which permits entrance to the professional fields. Without the degree, the doors to the professional fields are closed to you forever.

You may ask, "but I don't know what I want to be. Shouldn't I decide before I go off to college?'' That would be a serious mistake. You don't need a career goal in order to enter college. You don't even need to have a specific academic interest. In fact, once in college, you will have one or two years or even longer to test, to explore, to settle on a direction.

Remember, no matter which path you ultimately follow, they all start with the freshman year of college.

As further encouragement, here is a list of ten of the top growing occupational fields of the next ten years—all of which require two to four years of college:

- **Computer Science:** systems analysts, programmers, technicians.
- **Health:** nurses, doctors, dieticians, administrators.
- **Engineering:** mechanical, electrical, nuclear, civil.
- **Teaching:** kindergarten, elementary, science, math.
- **Money Management:** accountants, bankers.
- **Therapists:** occupational, physical, respiratory.
- **Law:** lawyers, legal assistants.
- **Resource Management**
- **Planning:** architects, surveyors.
- **Social Services:** psychologists, consumer advocates.

INTERACTION OF PERSONAL SKILLS AND KNOWLEDGE

How important is the interaction of personal skills and occupational knowledge? Ask yourself the following questions.

- Could you be a scientist without knowing how to gather information?
- Could you be an executive without knowing how to handle responsibility?
- Could you be a computer programmer without knowing how to analyze and solve a problem?
- Could you be a supervisor without knowing how to listen and see all sides of an issue?
- Could you be a lawyer without being able to speak articulately and persuasively?

Highly developed personal skills will allow you to succeed in whatever career field you choose. They will give you the flexibility to move quickly, even from one career to another if the field you have chosen turns out to be less fulfilling or challenging or rewarding than you thought. Maybe technological change is smothering the opportunities in your field. Your personal skills will flash you the warning signs, well in advance, and help you identify new opportunities. Personal skills will be your insurance for a rewarding life.

Personal skills will also allow you to advance in whatever career field you choose. The higher you rise, the more important these skills become. The top people in any organization accomplish their goals by working through people, not through things. They function by leading, by motivating, and by persuading.

WHAT ABOUT EARNINGS

College graduates earn more. That's a fact. We could publish long tables here, developed by the Census Bureau, that list lifetime earnings of high school dropouts, high school graduates, and college graduates, by age, by sex, by race.

But why waste space with tables? They show but one thing. Over a working life, a college graduate will earn $350,000 more than somebody who did not go to college.

That $350,000 will purchase a better home, nicer furniture, vacations, tickets to concerts and athletic events, improved medical care, and, an education for your children.

A NOTE TO THE WISE:
THE NUMBERS ARE IN YOUR FAVOR

You have heard of the baby boom in the fifties and early sixties, when over four million children were born every year.

That meant that eighteen or twenty years later, there were over four million people fighting for scarce college openings and job openings. The

economy couldn't absorb all the people who were reaching maturity each year. Many dropped out because there was no place for them to go.

You are fortunate. You are part of a much smaller generation. Now the college structure and the economy have more openings than there are people coming along. The colleges must go out and recruit and so must employers.

Look at the difference between 1960 and 1968: 4,250,000 births in 1960;

3,502,000 in 1968. That's nearly 750,000 people less. Is that a lot? You bet. Provided there was no traffic, you could lay them head to toe on the highway and they would reach from Washington, DC to Chicago, Illinois.

Because there are far fewer of you, you will be in greater demand and have more opportunities than your older friends. A better life awaits you. Think about that and take advantage of it.

OBSTACLES

We have made the case for college. We hope you are convinced. But being convinced and doing something about it may not be the same thing. You are probably thinking about obstacles now and, in your mind, these obstacles are higher and steeper than you can handle.

Not so.

Some of the obstacles exist only in your head. They include false beliefs and misconceptions about how hard it is to get into college and how there is no money to pay for it once you're there.

Some of the obstacles are caused by confusion about how to pick a college and apply for admission; what tests to take; what forms to fill out; when to do all these things and in what order. This is easily cleared up.

Some of the obstacles arise because you had not thought much about college until your senior year and therefore you didn't take some of the preparatory courses in your sophomore and junior years. These obstacles are real and we recognize that. But, at the same time, it is never too late. You may have lost some options, but plenty of others remain. There are special strategies for those who wait until the last second, strategies which will help you skirt the obstacles. The remainder of this booklet will:

- Clear your mind of false beliefs.
- Give you admissions and financial aid know-how.
- Outline special strategies for the late bloomers.
- Present a time table to keep you on track.

We know you can do it. So, read, learn, then do!

Chapter 4
Some Things You May Have Heard About College Just Aren't So...

You have to get rid of false beliefs about college. Too many students have walked into a cage of false beliefs, snapped shut the lock, and now can't get out.

How do we know about these false beliefs? Mrs. Slocum and Mr. Leider visited high schools in Chicago, Detroit, Los Angeles, New York City, and Washington, DC, to meet with hundreds of students and their counselors.

Typical questions we asked: Are you planning to go to college? Which college? Why that college and not another? Does college scare you? Why don't you want to go to college? Don't you think you can handle college work?

Some of the answers were inspirational. They left Mrs. Slocum and Mr. Leider "feeling good" about meeting so many sincere and earnest young people who wanted to improve themselves.

But some of the answers raised concern. They showed that there were some students who could not move forward. They were blocked by obstacles which they had constructed themselves.

The questions and answers which follow will help you to re-examine your priorities and overcome many of these false beliefs.

—PRIORITY #1—

"I want to start earning money now..."

A STUDENT:

Sure, I know about college. I have thought about it. But right now it's more important for me to find a job after graduating from high school and earn some real money. I don't want to wait any longer.

MRS. SLOCUM:

You won't have any trouble finding a job driving a truck or working in a warehouse or waiting on tables. And after you start work, you will make some money, certainly more than you make now.

But what about your future? The jobs you are talking about don't lead anywhere. Ten years from now, you will still be driving a truck or working in a warehouse or waiting on tables. And your take-home pay will not be much more than when you started. If you grumble about your pay, the boss can easily replace you with a younger person who is just starting out and who will work for less.

Your decision would make sense if that low-paying job was not going to be your lifetime occupation but a stop-out for a year or two, while you earn some money for college. But there are risks.

It is not easy to go back to study habits after a long interruption.

Also, you could pick up responsibilities, such as a husband or wife or baby, that may prevent you from returning to school. These kinds of responsibilities can easily lock you into that dead-end job.

My advice: it's best to go straight on to college, without any detours. Then, in four years, you will reap the bigger rewards of a college education. Be patient...

—PRIORITY #2—

"I've saved up some money. I sure want to buy a car..."

A STUDENT:

I've saved a couple of thousand dollars from part-time jobs. There is this car I really want, and I can get a good deal buying it. There is a lot I can do with a car.

MRS. SLOCUM:

I agree that there is a lot you can do with a car. But you can do even more with an education. A car will move you over a road. An education will move you through life. By choosing a short ride down the strip, you might forsake the big ride to a big future.

That's philosophy. But if philosophy doesn't grab you, try some numbers.

Say you have $2,000 saved up and use it to buy a car. What will the car be worth four years from now? $350?

Now invest that same $2,000 in a college education. What will that be worth four years from now? $350,000 in higher lifetime earnings.

So what will it be? $350 or $350,000?

—FALSE BELIEF #1—

"I can't afford college..."

A STUDENT:

I do want to go to college. But who will pay for it? My family can't afford it and there is so little financial aid....

MR. LEIDER:

Think again. In the coming school year, there will be over $20 billion in student aid—in scholarships, grants, work, and loan opportunities. The trick is in applying—that is, in applying correctly and in applying in advance of the deadlines. Read Chapter 6 with great care. It will teach you all the ins and outs of student aid.

But to put your fears at rest right now, I asked a number of financial aid officers to tell me how a student, whose family has no money whatsoever, can finance an education either at an expensive private college or at a less expensive state university. Their answer: it can be done through a combination of scholarships, work opportunities, and loans. Here are some examples that they provided just for you:

DAVIDSON COLLEGE, Davidson, NC
Annual Cost: $10,545

Scholarships/Grants	$ 8,045
Loans/Campus Work	$ 1,700
Student Summer Job	$ 800
TOTAL AID	**$10,545**

HAVERFORD COLLEGE, Haverford, PA
Annual Cost: $13,705

Scholarships/Grants	$10,455
Loan	$ 1,500
Campus Job	$ 750
Student Summer Job	$ 1,000
TOTAL AID	**$13,705**

STATE UNIVERSITY OF NEW YORK AT ALBANY
Annual Cost $5,050

Pell Grant	$ 1,900
NY Tuition Assistance	$ 1,375
NY Equal Opportunity Grant	$ 875
Supplemental Educational Opportunity Grant	$ 600
Student Summer Job	$ 300
TOTAL AID	**$ 5,050**

RUTGERS UNIVERSITY, New Brunswick, NJ
Annual Cost (State Resident) **$5,508**

Pell Grant	$ 1,900
NJ Tuition Aid Grant	$ 1,490
Educational Opportunity Fund	$ 600
Supplemental Educational Opportunity Grant	$ 400
National Direct Student Loan	$ 450
Student Summer Job	$ 668
TOTAL AID	**$ 5,508**

UNIVERSITY OF SANTA CLARA, California
Annual Cost: $9,450

State Scholarship	$ 3,400
Pell Grant	$ 1,775
University Grant	$ 1,961
National Direct Student Loan	$ 1,014
Work Study	$ 800
Private Scholarship	$ 500
TOTAL AID	**$ 9,450**

I could give more examples. From schools in the midwest and in the south. Public and private. From the historically black colleges. But I think I made the point. Aid is available.

There is, however, one troublesome area in the sample aid packages—and you probably noted it, too. That is the category called "Student Summer Job." What happens if a student can't find a summer job or couldn't work during the summer because he or she took make-up courses? Where will the summer earnings come from? The simplest way is to increase the loan component of the assistance offer. At Haverford, for example, the student without summer earnings might have to take a $2,500 loan instead of $1,500 loan. And that brings us to the next false belief: a mortal fear of loans.

—FALSE BELIEF #2—

"I don't want to go into debt to get educated..."

A STUDENT:

There may be aid, but most of it is in loans. I am scared to death of loans. What happens if I can't find a job after graduation? How can I pay it back then? And what will they do to me if I don't pay it back?

MR. LEIDER:

Relax. Student loans have features which don't make them scary.

There are three things you should know about student loans:

1. You don't pay anything on your loan—principal or interest—until six months after you have completed your studies. That gives you half a year to find a job and begin earning good money.

2. Inflation and pay raises work in your favor. As the years pass, your monthly loan repayments take smaller and smaller bites from your paycheck. That needs explaining. Say you must repay your loan at the rate of $50 per month for ten years. In the first year, the $50 may represent a day's pay. But five years from now, because of inflation and your now higher salary, the $50 becomes a half a day's pay. And ten years from now, $50 shrinks to two hours of work.

3. And if you can't find a job, you are still protected. You ask the lender for "forbearance." Forbearance means permission to (1) temporarily stop making payments or (2) extend the time for making payments or (3) make smaller payments than were scheduled. Typical reasons for forbearance: unemployment, poor health, deep personal problems.

Remember, long-term loans work in your favor. That's how you can finance a home, a business, an education—even a summer vacation. It's a technique that is based on confidence in yourself and in your future. It's a technique that you must learn to adopt.

—FALSE BELIEF #3—

"My hometown college may not be the best school but at least I can afford it..."

A STUDENT:

I can probably get a better education at another college. But if I enroll at my hometown college I can live at home and save on room and board. That leaves tuition, and my mother thinks she can swing it.

MR. LEIDER:

You shouldn't decide that a college is not affordable. Let the college tell you this. Always begin by picking the schools that are best for you in terms of course offerings, reputation, support programs, and other academic factors. Never start by picking schools on the basis of cost. Remember, if the school wants you, the financial aid office will find a way for you to pay. After you read the chapter on financial aid you will understand how.

—FALSE BELIEF #4—

"It takes high SAT scores to get into college..."

A STUDENT:

I've heard you need high SAT scores to get into college. I haven't taken the SAT. But I know that if I do I won't score high enough to win admission...

MR. LEIDER:

Let's talk honestly about the SAT, and when I say SAT I also mean the ACT—the admissions test produced by the American College Testing Program and used in the Midwest and the South.

The SAT does not measure intelligence, motivation, or creativity so it cannot predict your academic success. What it does seem to do is correspond closely to a family's income—the higher the income, the higher the scores.

That's one item of bad news. Now for another one: Many state university systems, like those in Texas and California, relate admissions to a numerical achievement standard that is based, in part, on the SAT and, in part, on a grade point average in academic subjects. Many private colleges also use SAT scores as admission cut-offs. Such colleges, to demonstrate that they are becoming "more selective," tend to raise the minimum scores required for entry.

So what can you do? Let me quote Mrs. Floretta McKenzie, the dynamic superintendent of the District of Columbia's Public Schools. She agrees that standardized tests contain bias. And, the only recourse, is *"to deal with it the way it is. They are not going to make up a new game for us."*

In "dealing with it" there is also some good news. Practicing for the SAT and getting coaching can improve scores. Your school may have a coaching course. If it does, enroll. If you can't find a course in your school, one may be sponsored by a neighborhood group or a church.

In the absence of a coaching course, borrow an SAT preparation book from the library and take practice tests. That will build your confidence. It will also help your vocabulary and sharpen your reasoning skills.

There is another bit of good news. There are admission officers who realize that the SAT contains cultural bias. They look for other qualities in an applicant—**determination, the ability to overcome adversity, a drive to succeed, and maturity.**

I asked a group of these progressive admission officers to draw for this booklet quick portraits of minority students who were accepted for personal qualities and potential, and not because of their SAT scores. All these students, incidentally, did well in college.

A CATHOLIC UNIVERSITY IN CALIFORNIA

Her family lives in a low-income, high minority area where few students graduate from high school and even fewer continue on to college.

She started high school with a heavy load of vocational courses. Eventually, she decided on a future in engineering. This required her to enroll in night courses and summer courses to make up on college preparatory work.

She demonstrated to us her willingness and determination to overcome linguistic and academic deficiencies.

She was granted admittance even though her SATs were a 390 verbal and 450 math. We felt this hard-working, self-determined young woman deserved a chance to fulfill her dream.

A LIBERAL ARTS COLLEGE IN PENNSYLVANIA

He was heavily involved in extracurricular activities, serving as president of the Puerto Rican cultural club and as a leader of several community organizations. He impressed us as an all-around student. We felt he was much stronger than his test scores. We decided the low scores reflected his bilingual background, and we did not give much weight to them.

A STATE UNIVERSITY IN THE SOUTH

The personal quality we most admired was tenacity. This student is black and comes from a foster home. The student has maintained a strong academic record while enduring family upheaval and separation from siblings. SAT verbal was 350...A very mature, articulate, and goal oriented person.

A MIDWESTERN UNIVERSITY

Daughter of a clerk at a steel company. Mother is unemployed. Fourth child in a family of seven. Secretary of senior class. Secretary of French club. Student Council. In her personal statement and essay she wrote about Dr. Martin Luther King and his dream of equality and how she sees some evidence of his dreams becoming reality. Her teacher described her as "intelligent...motivated...responsible...one who goes beyond what is expected or required."

A LIBERAL ARTS COLLEGE IN VERMONT

Son of separated parents, both unemployed, in a large northeastern city. The family life of this young man is not stable. Example: He went home one day, discovered that the family apartment had burned down and the family had moved and left no forwarding address.

He is the eldest of four children and the first in his family to attend college. His scores were a low 370 verbal and 370 math. However, his interviewer said, "Take him! He is not a 300+ verbal. He is very articulate and has a solid understanding of his self and the world around him. Confident in the most positive way. He's done a hell of a job considering his background!"

A MIDWESTERN UNIVERSITY

Son of a factory worker. Dropped out of high school his Junior year. He began his own reading program at home and took the GED exam for a high school diploma. SAT scores were 370 verbal and 430 math. In his interview he convinced the counselor that he had high personal goals and he worked well on his own. A highly motivated and very determined young man.

A PRIVATE UNIVERSITY IN CONNECTICUT

A young man from a background where his father is unknown and his mother is supporting the family as a bookkeeper. Apparently feeling his SATs were not strong enough, he submitted this bit of poetry for the consideration of the admissions committee:

I don't wish to be too wordy,
I'm not one to be verbose.
I want to say with candor,
I'm the man who has the most.

I'm intelligent and witty,
Realistic with foresight.
Responsible and pithy,
And if I might say, bright.

But my knowledge stretches past,
The score upon the test.
I'm always learning something,
And my grades will tell the rest.

I have hobbies to involve me,
Such as Art and Architecture.
Rubik's Cube and Crosswords,
In such things I find adventure.

My drive can be contagious,
My devotion quite delightful.
When I'm writing I'm courageous,
But my exaggeration's frightful.

So I can predict a future,
Where opportunities abound,
To develop every talent,
And to make those talents sound.

—FALSE BELIEF #5—

"One must take college prep courses starting in the freshman year of high school if one wants to go to college..."

A STUDENT:

They say I have to have four years of English, four years of math, and three years of science to go to college. Well, I didn't think about college until I started my senior year. There is no way I can make up all these courses in my last year of high school.

MRS. SLOCUM:

It's never too late. First of all, entrance requirements vary with each institution. A recent study concluded that while many colleges do require a college preparatory program for admission, a surprising number (especially state schools) only recommend one. You still may have to work harder now to make up lost ground—take some night courses and courses next summer. Or you may have to find a college with a strong developmental program (instruction in the academic subjects that you should have taken in high school, but didn't). But it is certainly not "too late." Another option would be to take the first year of college at a nearby community college or junior college where you can strengthen your academic preparation.

Remember, there are many routes that you can take, regardless of what you have done during your first three years of high school.

—FALSE BELIEF #6—

"I may be interested, but I'd like to talk to someone first, and I really don't know anybody who has gone to college. Nobody in my family has..."

A STUDENT:

I have a lot of questions about college. If I can get these questions answered, I might want to go to college. But my mother doesn't know anything about college and my older brother didn't go to college either. He joined the Army.

MRS. SLOCUM:

Every teacher in your high school is a college graduate. Your counselors are college graduates. The social worker is a college graduate. In the clinic, the doctors, nurses, and therapists are college graduates. If you walk up to any of these people and say, "I'm interested in going to college, but I have a few questions," nobody will say, "Beat it, I'm too busy." In fact, the people whom you ask will be flattered, delighted, and helpful. After you break the ice, don't ask just one person. Ask several. Some may favor big schools, others like small schools. Some will say stay close to home, others will suggest you go far away. Listen to all of them and watch your college knowledge grow.

"I am scared to go off somewhere where I don't know anybody and everybody there is different..."

A STUDENT:

I know everybody in my neighborhood. My friends are here. We understand each other without saying a word. But the college I am thinking about is a "white school." It scares me...

MRS. SLOCUM:

Until a few years ago I thought that we blacks were the only people who had experienced oppression. But then I took a course in ethnic studies at a local university and it was an eye opener to learn that other groups—the Irish, Poles, Jews, Indians, Chicanos, Latinos—had suffered like we had and struggled like we had. I discovered bonds that I had not thought possible and made many new friends.

But such an understanding takes time. It doesn't come immediately. I know what you are saying and your concern is a valid one. In reality, it may be difficult to adjust to life at a school that is far away or predominantly white. Initially, you may need the special support that only "your own kind" can give you. When looking over colleges, make it a point to find out whether it sponsors minority organizations, such as a black student union or hispanic student union. These minority organizations will provide the security and strength that come from togetherness.

Chapter 5

What You Need To Know About College Selection And Admissions

Buying a car is a lot easier than picking a college. There are no more than sixty different models to choose from—maybe seventy. You can test drive before making a final choice. And there is plenty of consumer advice around to balance the hype from the automobile manufacturers—advice on fuel consumption, repair frequency, safety features, warranties, and trade-in values.

But when you turn to college, you aren't dealing with sixty or seventy choices. It's like facing a showroom with over 3000 models. Only you can't try any of them out with a test enrollment, and consumer information is hard to find. Almost all college admission information is slanted because it is prepared by the colleges themselves. This information comes in all forms—fliers, posters, brochures, handbooks, catalogues, and laser disk presentations. One hardly knows where to start or what to believe.

Some colleges have familiar names. You know them because of the fame of their graduates or the power of their athletic teams. Others you know about because they are in your town or your state.

But most of the names will be new to you. What's behind these names? All kinds of schools. Big schools and small schools. Schools which are state or city operated and schools which are privately operated. There are schools which were founded by religious groups, and there are schools with no religious affiliation. In some schools, minorities are the majority. In others, minorities are represented by a much smaller percentage than in the population as a whole. Some are two-year colleges. Some are four-year colleges. Universities award graduate and professional degrees. Some schools are in urban settings, some are in the suburbs, and some are in rural areas. Some are in warm climates and some are where the winters are long and cold. Some are extremely selective, accepting no more than one of every ten applicants. Others have open admissions and accept all who apply. Some have rigorous application deadlines; miss one and don't bother to fill out the forms. Others use "rolling admissions" where you can apply at any time and are notified of acceptance or rejection as soon as your application is processed. Some schools are good in every department. Some have strong and weak departments. Sports are important in some colleges, but not in others. Some schools encourage fraternities and sororities. Others prohibit them. Some schools have only male students. Others accept only women. Most are co-ed.

Choices present problems for everyone. Making a choice becomes especially difficult if you have waited until your senior year to begin thinking about where you want to go. For many people, the process begins at a very early age. Mom and Dad have been thinking about the "right college" ever since their child started kindergarten. They themselves are usually college graduates. Their friends and relatives are college graduates. They have been buying books on college preparation and college selection. And, by the time their child enters high school, the choice of colleges has been narrowed to six or seven.

But what about you? Your parents may not have gone to college. There are probably no books at home about college preparation and college selection. You aren't able to drive around the countryside, visiting seven schools in seven states to find the school that is just right for you. On some days you don't even have the subway fare to check out Downtown University.

So what can you do? Three things. One—become even more determined in your drive to go on. Two—take the crash course on college selection and admissions which comes next in this chapter. And, three—after reading the chapter apply the "shortcut strategies" most appropriate to you. This will help you pick a handful of colleges with a good fit from the three thousand choices available.

CRASH COURSE: HOW HARD IS IT TO GET IN?

Look at the chart on the next page.

Few colleges have more than one applicant for each class opening. Most don't have enough applicants.

Of those that can pick and choose, a small handful gets as many as ten highly qualified applicants for each spot in the freshman class. Some 40 or 50 receive at least two applicants. Another 70 or 80 don't get two applicants, but they get enough applicants to reject some potential students who meet all entrance requirements.

The remaining 3000 + schools have more classroom spaces than applicants. That, however, should not lead you into thinking that you can get in, merely by paying an application fee.

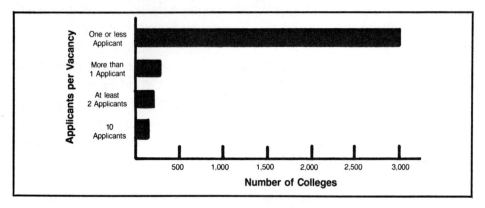

Most of these schools do have admission requirements which they spell out in their catalogues. Usually, there are three requirements:

One—the applicant must be a high school graduate.

Two—the applicant must have completed from 11 to 16 college preparatory units (also known as Carnegie Units). These may include four years (units) of high school English, two or three years (units) of mathematics, and the rest of the units in foreign languages, social sciences, and the physical sciences. (Remember to check with the school to find out if these units are required or recommended.)

Three—the applicant must achieve a satisfactory score on one of two college aptitude tests—the ACT or the SAT.

As a general rule, these are the admission requirements you will encounter:

ADMISSION REQUIREMENTS

HIGHLY SELECTIVE.

Two or More Applicants For Each Vacancy.
HS Graduation
High Class Standing
High Grade Point Average in College Preparatory Courses
High ACT/SAT Scores
3 Achievement Tests (tests which measure mastery of a subject)

16 Carnegie Units
Essay (which allows you to express your life goals)
Interview (can be conducted in your home town)
2 or More Recommendations
Community Service
Early Application Deadline— Often Sometime in January

COMPETITIVE.
More Than One But Less Than Two Applicants For Each Vacancy.
HS Graduation
High Class Standing
High Grade Point Average in College Preparatory Courses

High ACT/SAT Scores
14 Carnegie Units
Interview Recommended, Not Required
2 or More Recommendations
Early Application Deadline— Often February

AVERAGE.
Fewer Applicants Than Vacancies But Schools Adhere to Admission Requirements.
HS Graduation
Average Class Standing or Better
Passing Grades—Cs and Bs

Median ACT/SAT Scores
11 or 14 Carnegie Units
Recommendations Considered
Later Application Deadline— Could Extend to May or June

OPEN ADMISSIONS.
Accept All Qualified Students.
HS Graduation or Equivalent (GED Test)

College Will Test Applicant for Placement

Don't let these tables intimidate you into applying only to the schools with the least demanding admission requirements.

Some schools, as you will recall from the "SAT" discussion in the last chapter, are indeed unbending in their standards. But many more are flexible. They will insist that you meet all their admissions requirements, but your performance under each requirement is subject to an evaluation. In other words, if these schools say, "Take the SAT," you take the SAT. By not taking the test, you disqualify yourself from admission. But taking the test and not doing well does not necessarily mean rejection.

The admission officers at these schools—and they include public and private colleges—recognize that many minority students, because of special problems, are probably going to do much better in college than their records indicate.

You may not have been challenged. You may not have had the home support that builds self-esteem. You may not have been taught well. And you may have experienced problems with the cultural bias of standardized tests.

In your case, progressive admission officers will look for indicators other than the traditional yardsticks of class standing, grade point average, and ACT/SAT scores. They will look for drive and determination, tenacity and a desire to succeed, leadership and a sense of responsibility.

For this reason we say: Aim high on the collegiate selectivity ladder. Don't automatically head for the bottom.

Prepare for all the admission requirements. If they call for a test, register for the test. If they call for an interview, request an interview. If they call for recommendations, get recommendations. If they call for an essay, start writing. But PREPARE.

And then apply.

CRASH COURSE CONTINUED:
HOW MANY APPLICATIONS?

Smart gamblers hedge their bets. That gives them protection. They may not win as much; but at the same time, they limit their losses. No matter what happens, they don't get wiped out.

Smart college picking works the same way. You can't be sure that your first choice school will take you. And the fact that your application may be based on drive and personality rather than on high academic achievement and test scores adds to the uncertainty.

So what do you do? You also hedge. How? By applying to more than one school.

Here is what we suggest:
- Pick one or two schools where your chances of getting in are slim.
- Pick one or two schools where you have a fifty-fifty chance.
- Pick one school where the odds of admission are in your favor.
- Pick one school where you know for sure that you'll be accepted.

Apply to all of these schools. You may get accepted by the most selective school on your list. Or you may not. But you will get accepted somewhere—and that's what is important.

What about the rejections you pick up? Should you take these personally? Do you consider them as a blow to your ego? Of course not. Let's go back to the gambler. If he loses, do you think he develops doubts about his own judgment and tears his hair out? No. He recognizes that it's a game; and that in any game there must be winners and losers; and that today's losers may be tomorrow's winners.

He sees nothing personal in the turn of events. You shouldn't either.

CRASH COURSE CONTINUED: SHOULD I WORRY ABOUT COLLEGE COSTS?

Not at this time. Financial aid is available to cover most college expenses as long as you apply correctly, to the right agencies, and in advance of the deadlines.

Your greatest problem, at this time, may be with fees—something we have not yet talked about. You will find there are fees for taking the ACT and the SAT. Fees for taking achievement tests. Fees for college applications. Fees, later on, for filing your financial aid application. Besides these fees, there are additional costs. The cost of envelopes and stationery. The cost of making copies of all your applications. The cost of postage stamps.

You can request fee waivers. But these waivers won't cover everything. If you apply to several colleges—and you should—you may need as much as one hundred to two hundred and fifty dollars over a four month period, from September through January. That is a lot. We know it. We have a few suggestions that may help, and we'll share these with you in Chapter 8 of this booklet.

CRASH COURSE CONTINUED: IT'S IMPORTANT TO BE ORGANIZED

You must make every day count in the first semester of your senior year in high school. You will be "preparing" and "applying."

Preparing includes:

- Signing up for the right courses.
- Sharing your college plans with teachers and counselors.
- Registering for the tests you must take, building self-confidence for the tests, and then taking the tests.

- Identifying the teachers and counselors who will write your letters of recommendation.

   Applying includes:

- Gathering information about colleges.
- Identifying the schools that interest you.
- Filling out and mailing off the college application and financial aid application forms.

YOU'LL HAVE TO TAKE SOME SHORT CUTS

Ok, you say. I understand that time is short. I have lots to do. How can I quickly narrow down that list of 3000 plus schools to the six or seven that may be the best for me and my life goals?

The answer: You'll have to take some short cuts.

SHORT CUT STRATEGY: SOURCES OF COLLEGE INFORMATION

Where does one get information about colleges? Generally, there are four sources.

1. **People Who Have Been to College**—teachers, counselors. Stay a moment after class to talk to a favorite teacher. Make an appointment with a counselor. Tell them you want to go to college and ask for their recommendations.

Before giving you a recommendation, the teacher or counselor will probably want to know if you have made career plans, check into your course load and grades, ask about your preferences such as large schools or small schools, distant schools or close-by schools. Then they will give you their ideas. They may also suggest their own college. Have a pencil and piece of paper handy and take down their recommendations.

2. **College Directories.** College directories are of two types. There are the directories which record what the colleges say about themselves and

there are the directories which record what outside observers say about the colleges.

Examples of the first kind are the College Board's **College Handbook** and Lovejoy's **College Guide.** This kind of directory can come in book form or as a computer program.

The second kind of directory contains opinions about the colleges. It is important to remember that these are only opinions. The best is Cass and Birnbaum's **Comparative Guide to American Colleges.** In that category, you will also find books which evaluate colleges for their sensitivity toward special groups. Included here are Barry Beckham's **Black Student's Guide to Colleges** and the Feminist Press' **Everywoman's Guide to Colleges and Universities.**

You will need both types of guides. Those containing the college-provided information are good for basic facts—the size of the school, the majors it offers, the application deadline. The opinion guides will tell you about the school's strong points and weak points and make judgments about their sensitivity.

In searching for these directories, which are absolutely vital to your college plans, you will run into a problem. In our visits to dozens of high schools—and these are schools like you are attending now—we noted that neither the guidance offices nor the school libraries had good directory collections.

What to do? Find a friend who also plans to go to college. There is strength in numbers. The two of you visit the guidance office and the library and request that they purchase at least one college-prepared directory and one opinion directory. Will they do it? You bet they will. In fact, your interest and your knowledge of "titles" will please them.

3. College Fairs. In most large cities, the National Association of College Admissions Counselors (NACAC) and the National Scholarship Service and Fund for Negro Students (NSSFNS) stage a college fair. The groups rent an exhibit hall and then sell booth space to individual colleges. In each booth you will find a representative of the college's admission staff. He or she will have literature and handouts and can answer questions about the college and what it has to offer. These fairs attract colleges. It is not unusual to have as many as 1000 colleges renting booth space. The fairs are well publicized. Ask the guidance office about the dates. Also find out if attendance at the fair is an excused absence from school and whether the school can provide transportation to the fair. If enough students are interested, have a school bus take you to and from the fair.

4. Writing to Colleges. Colleges respond quickly to requests for information. If you write, you will get a handbook which describes course offerings, costs, and application procedures. Frequently, a postcard is included for you to use to get more information on a specific major or on financial aid or on housing.

Here is an all-purpose lettter, requesting college information:

Your Name
Street Address
City, State, Zip

Date

Director of Admissions
Name of College
City, State, Zip

Dear Director:

I will be graduating from (name of high school) in June (year).

I am interested in attending your college to further my academic and career preparation.

At your earliest convenience, could you please send me an admissions packet which includes information on academic programs, special services, costs, financial aid and housing.

Upon receipt of your information, I will correspond further with you or one of your admissions counselors regarding any specific questions that I may have.

I thank you for your attention to this request.

Sincerely yours,

(Your Signature)

SHORT CUT STRATEGIES: WHICH STUDENT ARE YOU?

You know now how to get college information. But you haven't yet picked that handful of schools, from the 3000+ available, on which to concentrate your efforts.

Our suggestions for doing this: Read the five student profiles we present to you. Determine which profile corresponds most closely to your situation. Then follow the "college-picking" strategy described for that profile:

PROFILE A—CAREER ORIENTED

You know exactly what you want to be. An accountant. A graphic artist. A systems analyst. A musician.

PROFILE B—UNSURE ABOUT CAREER

You are not sure what you want to be. You are still exploring your abilities and your options.

PROFILE C—NEEDS CULTURAL SUPPORT

You are immensely concerned about the transition to college—the move from the familiar to the unfamiliar. You believe the transition will be least painful if you can be with "your own kind of people."

PROFILE D—NEEDS ACADEMIC SUPPORT

You know you are smart, and you have a high regard for your abilities. But you are a realist and worry that your college preparation has been somewhat shaky.

PROFILE E—THE JOCK

You are a pretty good athlete. You believe you can use your body to broaden your mind.

COLLEGE SELECTION FOR
PROFILE A—CAREER ORIENTED

Your mind is made up, unshakably so. There is one career for you, and no other, and nothing can derail you from that goal. In that case, you want to go to a college which has a solid reputation in the field of your choice.

There are many advantages to finding such a college. The professors will be top experts in their field. They will have good connections with business and industry. And business and industry will have made scholarship money available to the school.

You may already know which colleges have developed national reputations in your chosen field.

But if you don't know, there are two things you can do:

1. Go to the Public Library and ask the reference librarian to locate a hefty book called Gale's **Encyclopedia of Associations.** Look up the name and address of the professional association which serves your intended career field. Then send a letter to the association's executive director. Let's say your aspiration is industrial engineering:

Your Name
Street Address
City, State, Zip

Date

Executive Director
American Institute of Industrial Engineers
25 Technology Park/Atlanta
Norcross, GA 30092

Dear Executive Director:
I am a high school senior who plans to enroll in college next year to major in industrial engineering. It is my understanding that many colleges have excellent programs in industrial engineering.
To help my in my college choice, I would appreciate it if you could provide me with a list of accredited schools which offer such a program.
I would also appreciate any advice you may be able to give me on choosing a school, as I am the first in my family to pursue this career.
I thank you in advance for your knowledgeable assistance in my educational planning.

Sincerely yours,

(Your Signature)

---

2. In the front of many college guides, such as Lovejoy's **College Guide,** you will find an alphabetical listing of college majors and the schools which offer them.

Either method will give you enough schools to form the basis of your college application list. You can further narrow the list using Profile B techniques (see below).

COLLEGE SELECTION FOR
PROFILE B—UNDECIDED ABOUT CAREER

If you are like most students, you haven't committed yourself to a specific career. You are still looking, testing, and exploring and plan to continue to weigh different possibilities while in college.

You are quite right in not rushing into a career choice. The first two years of college are usually devoted to the foundation subjects—English, languages, math, the physical and social sciences. It is not until the third year that you must declare a major field. That gives you plenty of time.

Your main concern should be that the school selected offers a range of majors. Then, no matter which direction you finally take, your academic goals will be met.

What's a good range of majors? It should include accounting, art history, business, communications, computer science, English, foreign languages, health areas (such as therapy or medicine), history, literature, mathematics, the physical sciences, psychology, sociology, and possibly music and theater.

Now you must pick schools that offer these majors.

Here is one way to create a list.

Give yourself a preference test on the topic, "What kind of college would I like to attend?"

Is it a college so close that I can live at home or one at some distance away, where I have to reside on campus?

If the college is at some distance, should it be in my state or can it be out-of-state?

What do I mean by distance? Under 250 miles? From 250 miles to 500 miles? More than that?

Where should my prefered college be? In a rural area? In a suburb? In a big city?

Where would I be most comfortable? In a small college (less than 2000 students)? In a mid-sized school (2000 to 5000 students)? In a large school (over 5000 students)?

Suppose you are a New Yorker, you have asked these questions, and you have answered them as follows: I want to go to a college away from home, but the distance should be under 250 miles. I would prefer to go out-of-state. I think I would be happiest in a big city, attending a large university.

On that basis, and using a map and a standard college directory, you would create the following list of schools:

Boston College
Boston University
Northeastern University
University of Massachusetts in Boston
Jersey City State College
Drexel University
Temple University
University of Pennsylvania
Towson State University
University of Maryland in Baltimore County
George Washington University
Georgetown University
Howard University
University of the District of Columbia

That was the first step. In the next step, you begin reducing the list to manageable size. How? By reading up on each of the colleges in a standard directory. If a college, based on this research, does not offer the complete range of majors or has admission requirements that you cannot possibly meet, you cross it off.

Then you narrow the list still further. You look up the remaining schools in one of the "opinion" directories. There you may learn that the editors are critical of a school's academic performance or consider it insensitive in its treatment of minority students. That research, too, can lead to some crossing out.

What's left becomes your application list.

We have prepared some worksheets which will help you to narrow your choices. These are found in Chapter 10.

COLLEGE SELECTION FOR
PROFILE C—CULTURAL SUPPORT REQUIRED

Ever notice how people enter a swimming pool? Some will take a flying dive into the water without first checking its depth or coldness. Others are more cautious. They'll look at the water, think about it, then stick a leg in and, if it doesn't get bitten off by a crocodile, another leg and then the rest of their body. There are the supercautious who sit on the edge of a pool silently cursing every child who splashes water their way before they finally lower themselves in, one inch at a time. And then you have all those who never dare to enter—they're the ones who miss the fun.

Moving from one culture to another is like going from dry to wet. It's easy or hard, depending on your background, your personality, and your level of self-confidence.

The fast learning pace at a college may provide enough shock without having the additional cultural strains of joining a "white society." You may well want to enter that fast learning pace without any additional strain.

How do you find colleges where your group has a sizeable representation? It's easy.

First, establish a general geographic area where you want to go to school, like New York State, Texas, Arizona, or Florida.

Then review the ethnic and racial composition of the student body at each school in the state, using a directory like Lovejoy's **College Guide.**

Say that you are Hispanic and your preference is for a college in Florida. Listed below are the Florida colleges with sizeable (10% or more) Hispanic student bodies:

Barry University
Biscayne College
Florida International University
Florida Memorial College
Ft. Lauderdale College
St. Thomas Villanova University
University of Miami

If your preference was for a school in Texas, you would find nearly 29 four year colleges with sizeable Hispanic student bodies. They include:

Bee County College
Del Mar College
Galveston College
University of Houston, Downtown
Pan American University
University of South Texas, Corpus Christi
University of South Texas, Laredo
University of Texas, El Paso
University of Texas, San Antonio
Victoria College

You can also find large Hispanic groups at *Truman College* in Illinois,

Atlantic Union College in Massachusetts, and the *College of Santa Fe* in New Mexico. This is by no means the end of the list—just a few names to get you started.

Now check the "personalities" of these schools in one of the opinion directories. Also check them for their range of majors and admission requirements. These checks will result in some crossing out. What's left is a manageable application list.

Here is an alternate way to search for schools which offer cultural support:

1. If you are female, scan **Everywoman's Guide to Colleges and Universities.**

2. If you are black, check Barry Beckham's **Black Student's Guide to Colleges.** Also, ask the Office of Public Information, US Department of Education, Washington, DC 20202 to send you a **roster of the historically black colleges and universities,** both public and private.

3. If you are Hispanic, ask **LULAC, 400 First Street, NW, Suite 716, Washington, DC 20001** for a list of colleges where Hispanic students will be present in substantial numbers.

COLLEGE SELECTION FOR
PROFILE D—ACADEMIC SUPPORT REQUIRED

You are smart enough to go to college. But for some reason or other, you got a late start. You didn't take all the academic subjects you should. You had bad instruction. You weren't challenged. Nobody ever mentioned college to you. And so you did not start to think about college until late in the game.

Well, it's never too late. But you will need help or you won't keep up with your better-prepared fellow students. The help comes from colleges in the form of pre-admission summer programs, reduced course loads, remedial instruction (such as writing and math clinics), the assignment of tutors, and the availability of special counselors who are familiar with students in your situation and can help you—as they have helped others before you—make the transition.

The College Board's **College Handbook** provides detailed information on the availability of special programs.

Say you are a resident of Houston. You have decided that you want to attend a public university within the state of Texas. The chart on the following page shows what you might learn about the special programs offered by the schools in which you are interested.

As you can see, some colleges have an entire range of programs; others do not. In looking at the schools, you will want to remember that special programs are a relative concept. Their job is to enhance an academic ability

	PRE-ADMISSION SUMMER PROGRAM	REDUCED COURSE LOAD	REMEDIAL INSTRUCTION	TUTORING	SPECIAL COUNSELOR
ANGELO STATE	X	X			
EAST TEXAS STATE	X			X	
LAMAR		X	X	X	
MIDWESTERN STATE		X			
NORTH TEXAS STATE				X	
SAM HOUSTON STATE					
SOUTHWEST TEXAS STATE	X		X	X	X
S F AUSTIN STATE			X		
SUL ROSS STATE		X	X	X	X
TEXAS A&I				X	X
TEXAS A&M	X			X	
TEXAS SOUTHERN				X	
TEXAS TECH	X	X		X	X
TEXAS WOMAN'S	X	X	X	X	X
U. OF HOUSTON		X		X	X
U. OF TEXAS, ARLINGTON	X	X		X	X
U. OF TEXAS, AUSTIN	X	X		X	
U. OF TEXAS, EL PASO			X	X	
U. OF TEXAS, SAN ANTONIO				X	X
WEST TEXAS				X	X

which is below that of the average student admitted. Thus, a student deemed to be in need of special work at a very selective institution might not require such "prepping" at a less selective school or at one that practices open admissions.

Therefore, you should not narrow down the schools by counting the number of special (remedial) programs available. Rather, you will have to decide for each school whether you have the intelligence, drive, and persistence to catch up with better prepared students.

Such a judgment may be difficult to make on your own. We do recommend that you sit down with the school counselor and seek his or her advice and recommendations.

You may also want to consider an alternative. That is: attend a nearby community college for a year, work hard, and then transfer to a four year institution.

Again, a discussion with your counselor is your wisest course.

COLLEGE SELECTION FOR PROFILE E—THE ATHLETE

The Reverend Jesse Jackson said once, *"Athletics teaches you to persevere beyond sweating and fatigue."*

But then he said, *"We can't just have skill with our bodies; we must develop our minds,"* and he told young people to *"practice math as assiduously as you practice jump shots."*

Be cautious about using your athletic abilities to ride into college. You may end up being used by coaches who take all your time to perfect your individual and team skills and leave you no time to develop your mind.

"So what," you may say. "I will have been scouted and signed to a contract by a major league team. Some players earn over one million dollars per year."

That's true. But for every Magic Johnson, Reggie Jackson, Tony Dorsett, and Fernando Valenzuela there are ten professional athletes who don't make giant sums of money or last very long in the majors.

In fact, only one out of every 12,000 high school lettered athletes will ever make money through athletic skills; of those, the average duration of their professional status is less than five years.

Unless you really are a budding superstar, we would say to you: go slow in capitalizing on athletic skills. Enjoy the competition and the sweat and the fatigue, but enjoy your mind even more. Use the other strategies to select a college.

And remember: this country needs thirty times as many accountants as professional athletes, and the typical accountant's career lasts six times longer than that of the professional athlete.

Summing It Up

1. Make sure your guidance office and high school library have current editions of the standard college directories—those that record information provided by the colleges and those that express opinions about the colleges.
2. Decide which of the college search strategies is appropriate for you.
3. Using that strategy—and the references—make a raw list of colleges.
4. Narrow down that list by evaluating the school's personality, the school's offerings and the school's admission requirements.
5. Prepare a final list of schools. Make sure the list includes at least one school that is a "safe bet" to accept you.
6. Discuss the list with your counselor.
7. Apply.

What's the time frame for doing all this? September through December of the senior year.

Chapter 6
What You Need To Know About Financial Aid

This is what you need to know about financial aid:

1. There is plenty of aid available to finance your education.
But:

- You must apply.
- You must apply correctly.
- You must apply on time.

2. There is nothing complex about applying for financial aid. Don't let anybody tell you differently.

3. Most financial aid, though not all, is awarded on a first-come, first-served basis. If you send your college applications off early, in December and January, you will have a good chance at the first-come financial aid programs. If you wait until late spring you may not get all the assistance you need.

4. Don't waste time on scholarship hunts. The pay-off isn't worth the effort. You have many more important things to do in your senior year than to look for scholarships.

5. Don't be afraid of loans. Without loans, you will find it hard to fund a college education. Uncle Sam, who stands behind most college loans, has taken the sting out of them. We talked about that in Chapter 4. You may wish to read that section again.

6. Read a good book on financial aid. The best: an annual guide called **Don't Miss Out** published by Octameron Press. Ask the guidance office or the school library to obtain the current edition.

THE PHILOSOPHY OF FINANCIAL AID

Your eligibility for financial aid is expressed as a monetary sum—in dollars and cents. It is the difference between what college will cost and what you are judged capable of paying.

For instance: if a college costs $10,000 and you are capable of paying $1,000, you are elibible for $9,000 in aid.

This is important: College costs are a variable. But the amount that you are capable of paying is constant. Let's attach numbers to that concept.

You are judged capable of paying $1,000 for college. You are considering College A which costs $3,000, College B which costs $5,000 and College C which costs $7,000.

At A you will be eligible for $2,000 in aid ($3,000–$1,000). At B your eligibility is $4,000 ($5,000–$1,000). At C it is $6,000 ($7,000–$1,000).

The lesson to be learned from this: *your out of pocket expense will be the same, whether you attend an expensive or a low-cost school. You don't save any of your own money by shopping for a cheap school.*

Incidentally, the amount of your aid eligibility is called your **Financial Need.**

THE COST OF COLLEGE

The cost of college usually includes seven elements:

1. **Tuition.**
2. **Fees,** such as lab fees.
3. **Books and Supplies.**
4. **Room.** Even if you live at home, an allowance is made for room costs. However, the allowance won't be as large as if you live on campus.
5. **Food.** Again, an allowance is made whether you eat at home or in the college cafeteria.
6. **Miscellaneous Expenses.** This category includes items like laundry money and medical insurance.
7. **Transportation.** If college is far away, transportation costs are based on two roundtrips home per year; if you are commuting, the costs include busfare or an automobile allowance.

Add these seven elements together and you have the cost of college which is used as the basis for determining your eligibility for financial aid. The cost, incidentally, is calculated by the college's financial aid officer.

WHAT YOU CAN PAY

The cost of college is one element of the financial aid formula. The other element is the amount of money your family is judged capable of contributing toward college costs.

How is that sum determined? From information you enter on the **financial aid application** (more about that form later). That information covers (1) your parents' income and assets and (2) your income and assets.

For many families, the formula will determine a zero dollar contribution to college costs from parental income and assets.

But now pay close attention: the formula assumes that you the student can chip in $700 to $1,000 from something called "summer earnings." It doesn't matter that you were unable to find a job or that you had to spend the summer in the classroom. The formula wants that $700 to $1,000. If you don't have it, the sum is shifted to your parents, even though the computer had just calculated a zero contribution for them.

So what can you do if you don't have the "summer earnings?"

One of two courses of action:

1. Bring the problem to the college's attention and request that the "summer earnings" figure be covered by other aid.

2. Suggest to the college that your loan be increased by the "summer earnings" figure.

Here is a sample letter that you can send to the college's financial aid officer at the same time you mail your financial aid application:

Your Name
Street Address
City, State, Zip

Date

Dear Director of Financial Aid:

I have applied for admission to your college and today sent my financial aid application to the processor.

I understand that the estimated family contribution which the processor will calculate contains an expected summer earnings figure. Unfortunately, I will not be able to work this summer. I plan to enroll in summer school. Also, my parents do not have the financial strength to absorb the summer earnings figure as part of their contribution.

It would be appreciated if the summer earnings figure could be waived in my case and covered with aid. If your policies do not allow that, I would be willing to accept a larger loan which incorporates the summer earnings figure.

I request that this letter be made part of my folder and reviewed at the time that you make your awards. Your consideration is appreciated.

Sincerely,

(Your Signature)

THE FORMS OF AID

The financial aid officer, after determining your college cost and subtracting from it your family contribution, calculates your aid eligibility.

Then an aid package is prepared, which—if you applied for financial aid correctly and on time—should, in most cases, cover your financial need.

Generally, the aid officer builds the package from three types of awards:

Grants and Scholarships. This money is given to you. It does not have to be repaid.

Employment Opportunities. This money you earn—usually at the minimum wage. The school will find you the job.

Loans. This money must be repaid. However, you don't pay interest on the loans while you are a student. And you don't have to start paying them back until six months after completing your college work.

If you are a little nervous about the first year of college and want to spend all your time studying, you can request that the school, initially at least, go easy on offering you work which may take time away from studies.

In that case, send this letter to the college financial officer:

Your Name
Street Address
City, State, Zip

Date

Dear Director of Financial Aid:

I have applied for admission to your college and I have also applied for financial aid.

During my freshman year, I plan to take full advantage of the developmental programs which you offer, to include tutoring, and special counseling.

These programs, as well as my regular course load, will take up all my available time. Accordingly, I hope that in my first year you can base all my aid on grants and loans.

After I have made the first-year adjustment, I know I will be able to accept work assignments as part of my aid package.

I request that this letter be made part of my folder. I appreciate your consideration.

Sincerely,

(Your Signature)

THE FINANCIAL AID APPLICATION

In most cases you will have to fill out from two to four different applications to link up with all major aid programs. The exact number depends on your home state and the programs available in your state.

You cannot submit the applications before January 1 of the year in which you will enroll in college (this is usually January 1 of your senior year of high school). The reason: the computers which analyze your application will want to know exactly how much your family earned in the preceding calendar year.

Here are some tips that are applicable to all financial aid forms:

1. **Apply as early as possible.** The early bird gets the worm.

2. **Take great care with the applications.** Follow the instructions exactly.

3. **Make sure income information on the application is the same as that which is reported on your family's federal income tax form.** The colleges may compare the two.

4. **Make copies of all your applications.**

5. Be aware that **if there is a change in family circumstances** after you have completed the application, you should **immediately advise the people who got the original form of the changes.** What are changes in circumstances? Unpleasant things like death, divorce, disability, job loss.

6. **If your parents are divorced or separated,** you report the income and assets of the parent with whom you lived the greater part of the time in the calendar year preceding the year of your college enrollment. You don't need to worry about the other parent.

7. **If the parent with whom you live remarries,** you will have to report the income and assets of your stepparent.

8. **If you don't have a social security number, get one now.** You will need it for the application.

9. **All the application forms you need will be available in the high school guidance office.**

10. **The counselors will be glad to help you** with filling out the applications.

11. **Pick up the applications in December** and, with your parents, spend some time during the Christmas vacation getting records ready so that you can fill out the forms and get them off right after the first of the year.

12. **It costs money to file some of the application forms.** Low income students can get a fee waiver. Ask the guidance office if you qualify for a fee waiver.

THE MAJOR AID APPLICATIONS

The first and most important application can have several names—the

Form	Name	Programs Which Are Tapped	Aid You Can Expect	First-Come First-Served
1	FAF FSS PHEAA SAAC	**Federal Pell Grant**	To $2,000	No
		Federal Campus-Based Programs Suppl Educ Oppty Grant Direct Student Loan College Work-Study	To $2,000 To $1,500 C. $800 (average)	Yes Yes Yes
		College's Own Resources	Varies	Yes
		State Student Assistance	Varies	Yes

FAF (Financial Aid Form), the **FFS** (Family Financial Statement), the **PHEAA** (Pennsylvania Higher Education Assistance Agency) or the **SAAC** (used in California). Which of the four applications do you use? The college to which you apply will tell you in its instructions.

This one application can link you up with four different programs.

How does one form do all of this? Here is how: the form goes to a processor. The processor determines how much your family can afford to pay for college. It forwards this information to the colleges you designate (the colleges to which you are applying). There, the information is given to the financial aid officer, and the financial aid officer goes to work, helping you.

Here are some notes on the programs:

The Federal Pell Grant. This program requires you to take an additional administrative step. After your application is processed, you will be sent a **Student Aid Report (SAR)** which indicates the size of your award. You will have to forward the **SAR** to the college where you plan to enroll.

The Campus-Based Programs are federal funds administered by the colleges. There are three programs. One is a grant. One is a loan. And one offers work opportunities. The grant (Supplemental Education Opportunity Grant) can be as much as $2,000 per year. The loan (National Direct Student Loan) carries a low 5% interest charge. You do not pay this interest until six months after you complete your college studies. You then have from five to ten years to repay the loan. The work opportunities (College Work Study) are pegged to the minimum wage or higher. Students who receive help under this program normally work from ten to fifteen hours per week.

The College's Own Resources. Some colleges have a lot of money. Others are not so well endowed. Generally, private colleges have greater resources, per student, for student aid than public universities. The help is usually in the form of scholarships and grants. It can also include loans from the college's own funds and employment opportunities which are in addition to the federal opportunities described earlier.

Form #2—The State Application

Form	Name	Programs Which Are Tapped	Aid You Can Expect	First-Come First-Served
2	State Application	**State Student Assistance**	Varies	Yes

State Student Assistance. Go visit your counselor now and get answers to these questions:

1. If I go to college out-of-state, can I qualify for assistance from my state? In some states you can, in most states you cannot.

2. Can I use the major aid application form to tap into my state's financial aid programs or will I need a special state form? Most state programs can be tapped with the major application form. But some states, like New York, require a special form.

If your state requires a special application, you will need to fill out a second form.

Form #3—Special Program Application

Form	Name	Programs Which Are Tapped	Aid You Can Expect	First-Come First-Served
3	Varies	**Programs for Disadvantaged Student**	Varies	Yes

Several States—Michigan, New York, New Jersey, California and others—have special assistance programs for economically disadvantaged students. Such programs may also be operated by large cities under the sponsorship of the mayor. Check with the guidance office to see if your state and your city have such programs, what the eligibility requirements are, and how one applies.

If there are such programs, and you are eligible, you will have to fill out a third application form.

If you have applied to colleges in December and January and sent off the major aid application form in January, you are on track. In March or April, you will receive a financial aid award letter from your intended college.

The letter will tell you (1) how much college will cost, (2) how much your family must contribute to that cost, and (3) how much aid, and of what kind, you will receive.

Form #4—The Loan Application

Form	Name	Programs Which Are Tapped	Aid You Can Expect	First-Come First-Served
4	GSL Application	**Guaranteed Student Loan Program**	To $2,500	No

If the family contribution includes an assumed $700 to $1,000 summer earnings, and you won't earn that amount, or if the aid package falls short of covering college costs, you will have to get a **Guaranteed Student Loan.** This takes another application form.

Guaranteed Student Loans are made by banks, savings & loan institutions, and credit unions. Your guidance counselor will know which institutions in your neighborhood make these loans. If the counselor doesn't know, ask the college financial aid officer.

Lenders are not hard to find. The reason: the loans are guaranteed by Uncle Sam. That makes them extremely safe, from the viewpoint of the lender.

The loans can be as high as $2,500 per year. The interest is 8%. However, you don't pay any interest while you are a student. Uncle Sam pays it. And repayment and interest do not start until six months after you complete your studies. You then have from five to ten years to pay off the loan.

NOTE: If your income is over $30,000, the maximum size loan is based on remaining need, but it can be no higher than $2,500 per year. Remaining need is a mathematical measure. It is calculated by subtracting your family contribution and any other aid you receive from the cost of college. Example: the college costs $6,000. Your family contribution is $3,000. You receive a $1,000 grant. Your remaining need is $2,000. $2,000 becomes the maximum size loan that you can receive.

Here is the "paperwork flow" on a Guaranteed Student Loan.

1. You pick up the application at a bank, S&L, or credit union.
2. You fill it out.
3. The bank—or you—forwards the application to your college's financial aid officer.
4. The financial aid officer (1) certifies on the form that you have been accepted and (2) specifies the maximum loan for which you are eligible.
5. The application is returned to the bank.
6. The bank makes the loan.

How long does this take? About eight weeks.

SOME CAUTIONS

All aid awards depend on "satisfactory academic progress." Each college has its own definition of "satisfactory academic progress," but generally, the term means that you must obtain passing grades in your courses.

50

If you don't have great study habits and are not sure how you will be able to handle the faster instructional pace at a college, you may not want to overload yourself with course work in your freshman year.

Students who bite off more than they can chew often lose their aid awards. Don't let it happen to you. Play it safe and go light.

Summing It Up

1. Obtain a social security number.
2. Find out which of the major aid applications—the FAF, FFS, PHEAA, or SAAC—is required by your college.
3. Pick up the application in the Guidance Office in December and begin assembling data that you will need to complete the form.
4. Send the form off as soon after January 1 as you can.
5. Find out from Guidance if you will need a separate "state application." If you do, get it and mail it in.
6. Also find out from Guidance if your state or city offers special assistance to economically disadvantaged students. If yes, obtain the application forms and mail them in.
7. Obtain a Guaranteed Student Loan—if required.
8. Never hesitate to ask your counselor for help.

Chapter 7
A Senior Year Time Table
For You To Follow

Month	Activity	Re-Read Chapter
September	Sign up for academic courses for the senior year.	
	Check inventory of college directories in School Library and Guidance Office. At the same time, meet librarian and counselors. Request purchase of references, if needed.	Chapter 5
	Visit nearest Public Library. Check college material.	Chapter 5
	Learn where nearest copying center is located.	
	Buy stationery.	
	Buy small pocket dictionary. Get in the habit of looking up every word that you don't understand. Use that word in three differenct sentences.	
	Obtain from Guidance Office the testing schedule for SAT, ACT, Achievement Tests. Write down the registration deadlines and the test dates. While in the office, ask for (1) policy on fee waivers and (2) copies of sample tests.	Chapter 5
	For the next six weeks, take one sample test every week.	

Month	Activity	Re-Read Chapter
October	Continue to take sample SAT tests.	
	Continue to use your dictionary.	
	Follow one of the strategies to narrow down your college list. By the end of the month you should have a list of likely colleges.	Chapter 5
	Discuss your college list with a counselor. Narrow the list again.	
	Write to the colleges you have selected for information and application materials. Use sample letter.	Chapter 5
	Register for tests.	
November	Continue to use your dictionary.	
	Take SAT or ACT and any other tests required.	
	Study material received from colleges.	
	Identify teachers and counselors who will write "college recommendations" for you. Discuss your college plans with them.	Chapter 5
	Check Guidance Office and library for financial aid reference **Don't Miss Out**, current edition. If available, check out and read. If not available, request acquisition.	Chapter 6
December	Continue to use your dictionary.	
	Send off college applications.	Chapter 5
	Obtain major financial aid form (FAF or FFS or PHEAA or SAAC) in Guidance Office.	Chapter 6
	Begin assembling data you will need to fill out financial aid form.	Chapter 6
	Find out from Guidance Office if special state student aid form is required. If yes, obtain form and become familiar with its requirements.	Chapter 6

Month	Activity	Re-Read Chapter
January	Continue to use your dictionary.	
	Mail off additional college applications.	Chapter 5
	Complete major financial aid form and mail off.	Chapter 6
	Complete state aid application, if required, and mail off.	Chapter 6
	If you won't have summer earnings, write letter to financial aid officers at colleges where you have applied.	Chapter 6
	Find out from Guidance Office if your state or city has special student aid program for economically disadvantaged students. If it does, obtain application form, fill out, and mail off.	Chapter 6
February	Continue to study hard.	
March/ April	You will receive acceptances/rejections from colleges to which you applied. You will also receive, from these colleges, financial aid award letters.	Chapter 5 and Chapter 6
	Discuss your options with counselor.	
	Continue to use your dictionary.	
May	Make decision on college acceptance and on financial aid award letter. Respond to school with your acceptance.	Chapter 5 and Chapter 6
	Advise other schools which accepted you of your plans. Remember there are students on waiting lists hoping to get into these schools.	
	If needed, identify local lenders under the Guaranteed Student Loan Program. Obtain loan application, fill out, and send to college for certification.	Chapter 6
	Make summer plans. Employment or summer school.	
	Continue to use your dictionary.	

Month	Activity	Re-Read Chapter
June	HS Graduation	
September	**Start college. Congratulations.** **You are on your way!**	

Chapter 8
Application Fees, Resources, Writing Letters, Helpful People, Helpful Addresses . . .

APPLYING FOR COLLEGE COSTS MONEY

Before you begin to worry about pre-college costs, talk to your counselor about fee waivers. You should qualify for waivers on testing fees and the financial aid form processing fees. You might also get colleges to waive their application fee, or cover this fee with financial aid.

The estimate below represents the "worst case." In other words, the maximum amount of money you will have to spend on fees and minor expenses in your senior year. This assumes no waivers were obtained:

Item	Month				
	Sept	Oct	Nov	Dec	Jan
Buy a dictionary	4.00				
Buy stationery	3.00				
Copying		1.00	1.00	3.00	3.00
Aptitude Test		11.00			
Achievement Tests (3)		54.00			
Mailing Test Scores to Colleges		20.00			
College Applications				60.00	60.00
Financial Aid Applications					20.00
Postage		2.00	2.00	3.00	3.00
TOTAL	**7.00**	**88.00**	**3.00**	**66.00**	**86.00**
GRAND TOTAL					**250.00**

Here is how you might budget for these expenditures. Start with a $75.00 kitty and add $35.00 per month to your college application fund. Such a plan would produce the following cash flow:

Month	Add	Spend	Month-End-Balance
Sept	$35.00	$ 7.00	$103.00
Oct	$35.00	$88.00	$ 50.00
Nov	$35.00	$ 3.00	$ 82.00
Dec	$35.00	$66.00	$ 51.00
Jan	$35.00	$86.00	$ 0

Remember, this is an illustration of the "worst case." If you are successful in obtaining all of the fee waivers, you need only spend $25.00, or $5.00/month!

RESOURCES

The guidance office and/or the library should have the following resources. If they don't, request that they obtain them. You will certainly need them to carry out your college selection/admission/financing plans in an informed manner:

Directories Which Include College Supplied Information:

1. *College Handbook*, current edition, published by the College Board.

2. *Guide to Undergraduate Study*, current edition, published by Peterson's Guides.

3. *Lovejoy's College Guide*, current edition, published by Simon & Schuster.

Directories Which Contain Evaluations of Colleges:

1. *Comparative Guide to American Colleges*, current edition, published by Harper & Row.

2. *Everywoman's Guide to Colleges and Universities*, published by the Feminist Press.

3. *Black Student's Guide to Colleges*, published by E.P. Dutton.

Financial Aid Guides:

1. *Don't Miss Out: The Ambitious Student's Guide to Financial Aid*, current edition, published by Octameron Associates.

2. *College Grants From Uncle Sam*, current edition, published by Octameron Associates.

3. *College Loans From Uncle Sam*, current edition, published by Octameron Associates.

4. *Minority Organizations: A National Directory*, current edition, published by Garrett Park Press.

SECONDARY RESOURCES

Directories Which Contain Scholarship Information:

1. *Career Development Opportunities for Native Americans*, free from the Bureau of Indian Affairs.

2. *Directory of Financial Aids for Women*, current edition, Reference Service Press.

3. *Financial Aid for Minorities in Allied Health*
Financial Aid for Minorities in Business
Financial Aid for Minorities in Education
Financial Aid for Minorities in Journalism and Communications
Financial Aid for Minorities in Law
Financial Aid for Minorities in Science
Financial Aid for Minorities in Medicine
Financial Aid for Minorities in Engineering
All published by Garrett Park Press.

WRITING LETTERS

Throughout the text we included sample letters that can serve as models in requesting information or in letting you influence decisions made about you. Type your letters, even if this means getting help from someone at your high school. If you absolutely must write by hand, make sure you use a black pen and print neatly.

"Obtaining Career Information" (Chapter 5)
"Requesting College Application Information" (Chapter 5)
"Seeking Aid to Replace a Non-Existent Summer Earnings
Contribution" (Chapter 6)
"Influencing the Composition of the Aid Package" (Chapter 6).

HELPFUL PEOPLE

Teachers
Guidance Officers
School Librarians
Public Librarians
Ministers and Religious Leaders
Civic Group Leaders

HELPFUL ADDRESSES

Aspira of America
205 Lexington Avenue
New York, NY 10016

Aspira offers free counseling, and scholarship and loan information to Puerto Rican Students.

League of United Latin American Citizens (LULAC)
National Education Service Centers, Inc.
Suite 716, 400 First St., NW
Washington, DC 20001

LULAC offers counseling for low-income students and maintains a scholarship fund for Hispanic students.

National Council of La Raza
c/o Gaudalupe Saavedra
Vice President for Special and International Projects
Suite 200
1725 Eye St., NW
Washington, DC 20006

The National Council provides sources of financial aid to Hispanic students.

National Scholarship Service and Fund for Negro Students
562 Third St.
Brooklyn, NY 11215

NSSFNS provides free counseling and referral service for all minority students.

Office of Indian Education Programs and Bureau of Indian Affairs
18 and C Streets, NW
Washington, DC 20245

BIA provides scholarship and loan information to Native Americans.

Chapter 9
Worksheets

I. WHAT KIND OF SCHOOL WOULD I LIKE TO ATTEND?

II. MY COLLEGE INFORMATION CHECKLIST

After you read this book and fill out Worksheet I, you should have a pretty goood idea of what kind of college or university you want to attend. Now you must find the school which meets all of your requirements.

The next few pages will help. Use these forms to guide you as you look through college handbooks. When you find a school that looks like it might be right for you, read its description carefully, and take notes. Use a separate form for each college. When you're done, you will have a fairly complete profile of each school, and you're ready to move on to Worksheet III.

III. MY APPLICATION DEADLINES CHECKLIST

Now that you've decided on a list of schools, it's time to start keeping track of all the due dates and deadlines. Worksheet III will keep you on time. Make a copy of Worksheet III for each school to which you apply.

I.	Criteria	Sample Answer	My Preference
	Location?	Baltimore, Boston, New York, Philadelphia, Washington	
	Type of School?	Four Year	
	Size of School?	Over 5000	
	Large minority Population?	Yes	
	Majors Offered?	All	
	Athletic Programs?	Football, Track	
	Health Services?	All services	
	On-Campus Housing?	Coed Dorms	
	Special Academic Programs?	Tutoring	
	Student Activities?	Black Student Union, College Newspaper	
	Other?	No religious affiliation, Coed	

Name of School: _____

Address: _____

Type of College (check):   ☐ Four Year   ☐ Two Year
Religious Affiliation (check):   ☐ Yes   ☐ No
Student Body Size: _____ Men   _____ Women

Enrollment

Asian	_____%	Black	_____%
Foreign	_____%	Hispanic	_____%
White	_____%	Nat. American	_____%

ADMISSION REQUIREMENTS

1. High school graduation required?(check)   ☐ Yes   ☐ No
2. GED accepted? (check)   ☐ Yes   ☐ No
3. Required tests? (check)   ☐ Yes   ☐ No
   ☐ SAT   ☐ ACT   ☐ Achievement
4. Application fee—can it be waived?(check)   ☐ Yes   ☐ No
5. Remedial programs offered? (check)   ☐ Yes   ☐ No
6. Interview required? (check)   ☐ Yes   ☐ No
   If yes, are off-campus interviews possible?
   (i.e., in your home town) (check)   ☐ Yes   ☐ No

COLLEGE COSTS

1. Tuition $_____
2. Room & board $_____
3. Other fees $_____
   TOTAL $_____
4. What kinds of scholarships/grants/loans are available? (check)
   ☐ PELL   ☐ SEOG   ☐ NDSL   ☐ GSL
   ☐ CWS State Scholarships/Grants
   ☐ University Scholarships/Grants
   ☐ Private Scholarships/Grants
5. Special application for state money? (check)   ☐ Yes   ☐ No

STUDENT LIFE

1. Student activities (check those which are offered)
   ☐ Newspaper/Magazine/Radio   ☐ Yearbook
   ☐ Music/Drama Group   ☐ Debate Team
   ☐ Religious Groups   ☐ Cultural/Ethnic Groups
   ☐ Other
2. Housing (check those which are offered)
   ☐ Women's Dorm   ☐ Men's Dorm
   ☐ Coed Dorm   ☐ International House
   ☐ College Owned Apartments   ☐ Married Student Housing
   ☐ Special Interest Housing   ☐ Fraternities/Sororities
3. Athletic programs (list all that interest you)

Intercollegiate Programs   **Intramural Programs**

_____   _____

_____   _____

Name of School: _____

Address: _____

Type of College (check):	☐ Four Year	☐ Two Year
Religious Affiliation (check):	☐ Yes	☐ No
Student Body Size:	_____ Men	_____ Women

Enrollment

Asian	_____%	Black	_____%
Foreign	_____%	Hispanic	_____%
White	_____%	Nat. American	_____%

ADMISSION REQUIREMENTS

1. High school graduation required?(check)   ☐ Yes   ☐ No
2. GED accepted? (check)   ☐ Yes   ☐ No
3. Required tests? (check)   ☐ Yes   ☐ No

   ☐ SAT   ☐ ACT   ☐ Achievement

4. Application fee—can it be waived?(check)   ☐ Yes   ☐ No
5. Remedial programs offered? (check)   ☐ Yes   ☐ No
6. Interview required? (check)   ☐ Yes   ☐ No
   If yes, are off-campus interviews possible?
   (i.e., in your home town) (check)   ☐ Yes   ☐ No

COLLEGE COSTS

1. Tuition $_____
2. Room & board $_____
3. Other fees $_____
   TOTAL $_____
4. What kinds of scholarships/grants/loans are available? (check)
     ☐ PELL   ☐ SEOG   ☐ NDSL   ☐ GSL
     ☐ CWS State Scholarships/Grants
     ☐ University Scholarships/Grants
     ☐ Private Scholarships/Grants
5. Special application for state money? (check)   ☐ Yes   ☐ No

STUDENT LIFE

1. Student activities (check those which are offered)
     ☐ Newspaper/Magazine/Radio   ☐ Yearbook
     ☐ Music/Drama Group   ☐ Debate Team
     ☐ Religious Groups   ☐ Cultural/Ethnic Groups
     ☐ Other
2. Housing (check those which are offered)
     ☐ Women's Dorm   ☐ Men's Dorm
     ☐ Coed Dorm   ☐ International House
     ☐ College Owned Apartments   ☐ Married Student Housing
     ☐ Special Interest Housing   ☐ Fraternities/Sororities
3. Athletic programs (list all that interest you)

Intercollegiate Programs	**Intramural Programs**
_____	_____
_____	_____

Name of School _____ **III.**

Admissions Deadline _____

Priority Date _____

Closing Date _____

Financial Aid Deadline _____

Priority Date _____

Closing Date _____

- -

	Date Due	Date Sent
Application Form	_____	_____
Application Fee	_____	_____
Essay	_____	_____
High School Transcript or GED Results	_____	_____
TEST SCORES		
SAT	_____	_____
ACT	_____	_____
Achievements	_____	_____
Other	_____	_____
Letters of Recommendation	_____	_____

_____ _____ _____ _____
NAME   DATE REQUESTED

_____ _____ _____ _____
NAME   DATE REQUESTED

	Date Due	Date Sent
Interview (if required)	_____	_____
Campus Visit (if required)	_____	_____
Financial Aid Form	_____	_____
Other	_____	_____
Achievements	_____	_____
Other	_____	_____
Letters of Recommendation	_____	_____

Name of School _____

Admissions Deadline _____

Priority Date _____

Closing Date _____

Financial Aid Deadline _____

Priority Date _____

Closing Date _____

- -

	Date Due	Date Sent
Application Form	_____	_____
Application Fee	_____	_____
Essay	_____	_____
High School Transcript or GED Results	_____	_____
TEST SCORES		
SAT	_____	_____
ACT	_____	_____
Achievements	_____	_____
Other	_____	_____
Letters of Recommendation	_____	_____

_____   _____   _____   _____
NAME   DATE REQUESTED

_____   _____   _____   _____
NAME   DATE REQUESTED

Interview (if required)	_____	_____
Campus Visit (if required)	_____	_____
Financial Aid Form	_____	_____
Other	_____	_____
Achievements	_____	_____
Other	_____	_____
Letters of Recommendation	_____	_____

Chapter 10
Meet the Authors of This Booklet:
They Weren't Born With a Silver Spoon

Robert Leider

"...no matter how bad your start, you can create a rewarding life for yourself..."

What's a middle-aged white guy doing, advising young minority students, you may ask.

Mr. Leider's response:

"I know about adversity. And I know that you don't have to be black or brown or yellow to experience discrimination. It happens to whites too.

"I was born in Europe. When I was a small boy, the Nazis invaded my country. They let me know, very quickly, that I practiced the wrong religion.

"They made me sew a yellow star on my clothes. After I wore the star, I could no longer go to school. Or anywhere else. Anybody who saw me had the right to curse me or kick me or hit me or spit on me. And I wasn't allowed to complain.

"Later, the Nazis got rougher. I was put in a sealed freight car and shipped to a concentration camp. There, people were killed by the hundreds, every day. After they were dead, their hair was cut off to be sold and their teeth were kicked out and checked for gold fillings.

"I was lucky. I lived.

"I came to the United States when I was fifteen years old. I spoke no English. I could hardly read or write. And I was hungry. I still remember my first day in New York and a stop at a cafeteria. I could not understand how people could leave so much food on their trays.

"Who helped me? A counselor. A wonderful woman named Elizabeth McGrath. She made sure I learned English. She introduced me to the school library and a world of books. She put me in the right courses.

"I took it from there. I went to college. First, I studied engineering. Then I shifted to literature and the social sciences. I became a researcher and then a writer and, finally, a book publisher.

"Today I am pleased when people say 'Oh, Mr. Leider, I am so glad to meet you. I have read one of your books.'

"But that pleasure is small compared to my joy in the United States in a land of opportunity where, no matter how bad your start, you can create a rewarding life for yourself.

"I did. Now I want to help others achieve the same thing."

Dorothea Slocum

She has spent all her life reaching back and helping others strive for an education.

When Mrs. Slocum was younger, most women did not attend college. But she did. And she did not stop at graduation. She obtained advanced degrees.

Since then she has spent all her life reaching out and helping others strive for an education. Her emphasis: reading and a love of books. Her files are filled with letters from people whose eyes and hearts she opened to these pleasures.

Mrs. Slocum is a reference librarian with a specialty in "young adult services." But her activities have gone far beyond a neighborhood public library.

She belongs to the International Reading Association—a 65,000 member organization of professionals engaged in teaching reading, improving reading habits, and raising literacy levels throughout the world. Within the Association, she has served as secretary, treasurer, and chairperson of the Storytellers' special interest group.

She has chaired the District of Columbia Council of Librarians, served as a docent at the Folger Shakespeare Library in Washington, DC, and is a member of the National Council of Teachers of English.

Another of her many accomplishments has been the organization of an annual "Operation College-Bound"—a higher education fair in Washington's Southeast neighborhood—where students, parents, teachers, counselors, and college admissions officers meet and exchange information.

Mrs. Slocum's eyes shine when she tells stories about the many people who were motivated by Operation College-Bound to go on to college and become successes. "Oh, yes," she will say. "When I first met Patricia, she wasn't even thinking about college. Tomorrow she is graduating from Fordham Law School with highest honors..."

Mrs. Slocum is somebody. She has helped others to become somebody. She knows it can be done.

Chapter 11
A Last Thought

A vendor was selling balloons on the streets of New York. When business slowed down, he would release a balloon.

As the balloon rose toward the sky, a fresh crowd of buyers gathered around him and business would pick up for a few minutes.

The vendor alternated the colors of the balloons he released, first a red one, then a white one and later a yellow one.

After a while, a little girl tugged at his sleeve, looked him in the eye, and asked, "Mister, if you release a black balloon, would it go up?"

The vendor said without hesitation, "Little girl, it's what is inside those balloons that makes them go up."

Acknowledgements

The staff of Educational Access would like to thank the following college admissions and financial aid officers for providing us with sketches of students who have succeeded and sample financial aid packages for students from disadvantaged backgrounds:

Robert L. Baily
Director of Admissions, University of California, Berkeley.

Michael C. Behnke
Dean of Admission, Tufts University.

William R. Bennett
Director of Financial Aid, Cleveland State University.

George C. Brooks
Director of Financial Aid, University of Missouri at Columbia.

Kathleen Bush
Admissions Office, University of Detroit.

Richard Cashwell
Director of Admissions, University of North Carolina at Chapel Hill.

Catherine E. Clack
Assistant Director of Admissions, Rice University.

Evelyn B. Finck
Associate Director of Undergraduate Admissions, Rutgers University.

David M. Flynn
Dean of Admissions, Fairfield University.

Vernon L. Francis
Assistant Director of Admissions, Haverford College.

John V. Griffith
Dean of Admissions and Financial Aid, Davidson College.

Rodney A. Hart
Director of Admissions, State University of New York at Albany.

Thomas B. Martin
Director of Admissions and Financial Aid
Beloit College.

James J. Scannell
Dean of Admissions and Financial Aid, Cornell University.

Richard C. Skelton
Director of Admissions, Bucknell University.

Sylvia V. Terry
Assistant Dean of Admissions, University of Virginia.

Richard J. Toomey
Director of Student Records and Financial Services
University of Santa Clara.

Elizabeth G. Vermey
Director of Admissions, Bryn Mawr College.

Phyllis Washington-Stone
Admissions Counselor, University of Notre Dame.

Jimmy Williams
Associate Director of Admissions, Middlebury College.

We would also like to thank the following high school counselors and administrators for their invaluable assistance:

Linden Beckford
Washington Prep High School, Los Angeles, CA

Queen Boyd
Dunbar High School, Washington, DC

Carolyn Briscoe
Pershing High School, Detroit, MI

P. Drummond
Northern High School, Detroit, MI

Starleen Hamme
Pershing High School, Detroit, MI

Phyllis Hart
Banning High School, Wilmington, CA

Gwendolyn Hoover
Cardoza High School, Washington, DC

Dr. Phillip Jeunette
Anacostia High School, Washington, DC

Eleanor Jones
Director of Guidance, Detroit Public Schools

Annette Levey
Julia Richman High Schook, New York, NY

Barry Liebman
Martin Luther King High School, New York, NY

C. McClintock
Western High School, Detroit, MI

Carolyn Milam
Cardoza High School, Washington, DC

Lorraine Monroe
Department of Studies, Brooklyn, New York

Don Mrsocak
Garfield High School, Los Angeles, CA

Clarence Nemhardt
Cardoza High School, Washington, DC

Florence Ridley
Guidance & Counseling, DC Public Schools, Washington, DC

Eva Rousseau
Dunbar High School, Washington, DC

Cheryl Rutherford
Lindblom Tech High School, Chicago, IL

Nancy Scott
Prospect Heights High School, Brooklyn, NY

Allen J. Smith
Bureau of Guidance, Board of Education, Chicago, IL

Tony Solorzano
Bell High School, Bell, CA

Jesus M. Sosa
Bureau of Guidance, Board of Education, Chicago, IL

B. Weavers
Martin Luther King High School, Chicago, IL

Jack Wright
Franklin High School, Los Angeles, CA